This book belongs

We Believe For Kids!

Quarter 1

Who is God?

Student's Journal

We Believe For Kids!

Rev. Randall A. Bach, General Editor
Dr. David L. Cole, Theological Editor
Rev. Andrea P. Johnson, Copy Editor

Copyright © 2021 by OBC Publishing
Published in Des Moines, Iowa, by OBC Publishing

Color version ISBN: 978-1-7373442-2-3
B&W version ISBN: 978-1-7373442-3-0

Printed in the United States of America.

Contents

Acknowledgments

Teachers, we appreciate you! You understand the importance of investing your time into our children, giving them a sound spiritual basis by which they can develop an informed, faith-filled worldview. Your dedication will help steer the course of their lives.

We are indebted to a team of knowledgeable, dedicated children's workers, youth workers, and other leaders with a wealth of experience in teaching and leading student ministries who voluntarily worked diligently to help envision, craft, and write the curriculum for *We Believe For Kids*. They are:

Rev. Randall A. Bach   Kelly Loftis
Rev. Hannah J. Bemis   Claudine Morgan-Lewis
Rev. Chris Cavan   Rev. Kevin Starkey
Rev. Candi Hagan   Taylor Van Sickle
Rev. Andrea Johnson

We also appreciate the many people who have made this book a reality. We offer a huge "thank you" to **Nicole Kerr**, our creative assistant, for her immense contributions, including creating the *Student's Journal* and for contributing to the graphic design and layout. Her imaginative and administrative skills have driven and shaped this entire process from its inception to its completion. We also want to call out **Hannah Bemis**, for the hours she spent proofreading in addition to hours of writing. We are also grateful to **Greg Roberts**, Open Bible's print media manager, for graphic design, layout, and publishing research.

We want to credit **Lucas Hansen** for the cover and book design concept and **Paula Hernández**, a freelance illustrator and concept artist with Boomi Art, for creating our superhero mascots, Centro and Nora.

Finally, we thank churches like yours that recognize the fact that we have a huge opportunity and responsibility to communicate to our young people the importance of living out their faith in Christ and to give them tools to do so. May God continue the work He has called you to do.

Randall A. Bach, David L. Cole, and Andrea P. Johnson

V

Introduction

Have you thought about why you do some of the things you do, why you make some of the choices you make, or support some of the causes you support?

Social media, your teachers, your parents, and others are all trying to tell you what to do; they even try to tell you how to think! Some of those voices are pretty loud, and they don't always agree. How do you know which of these voices to listen to? Are you one that follows the crowd, or do you like to think things through on your own?

You may have heard of **The Emperor's New Clothes**, a folktale written by Hans Christian Andersen. In the story a couple of swindlers manage to talk a vain emperor into buying expensive clothing from them that is supposedly invisible to those who are "stupid" or "incompetent." The emperor loves the idea, and the fraudsters proceed to display what they describe as exquisite bolts of cloth with which they pretend to create elaborate clothing.

Of course the whole thing is a hoax, but the emperor does not let on that he cannot see the clothing because he doesn't want people to think he is incompetent. All the townspeople as well ooh and aah over the clothing because they too fear being thought of as inept. In the end, the emperor is left parading before the whole village in nothing but his underclothes!

Sadly, this scenario has played out in much of our society today. Many people try to get us to go along with the crowd and to follow the latest trends even though those trends may be wrong. The emperor may have believed he was wearing fine clothing, but in reality, he was nearly naked. We too may want to believe certain things are true but that does not make them true, even if everyone else thinks they are.

That's why it is important that you know what truth is. Real truth does not change. Real truth helps us make right decisions. More important, real truth leads us to God.

We want to help you discover truth. That's why we are so excited to share with you *We Believe For Kids!* This course will help you answer questions such as "Who is God?" "Who Am I?" and "Why Am I Here?" This course is designed to present you with information that will help you make your own decisions about what you believe, and to make those decisions based on truth. This journal will help you remember the information you are taught and also provide a place to record your own thoughts and opinions. We encourage you to keep it even after you have completed the course as a way to look back and remember your thought processes at this time.

More than anything, we trust that you will use this class time to deepen your relationship with God. He really wants to spend time with you!

Randall A. Bach, David L. Cole, and Andrea P. Johnson

We Believe For Kids!

Lesson 1

The Bible

Big Question:

Why should I believe the Bible?

What We Believe:
(Doctrinal Statement)

We believe the Bible is God's Word; it is truth. It serves as a trustworthy guide to our everyday lives.

Key Verse:
Write out the key verse in the space below.

2 Timothy 3:16

The Bible

Discussion Questions:
Get your pencils ready!

What are your favorite books, or movies that came from books, and why?

What are some movies based on true stories?

Lesson 1

Going Deeper:

Doctrine: something we _____ that is based on what the _____ says.

Each year _____ _____ copies of the Bible are sold! The Bible is the best-selling book of the year, every year!

Did You Know?

Diary of a Wimpy Kid - sold over 200 million copies
Narnia - sold over 100 million
Lord of the Rings - sold over 150 million
Harry Potter - sold over 500 million

But the Bible is the best-selling book of the year EVERY YEAR!

Christians believe the Bible is 100% the creation of human authors but also 100% inspired by God!

[answers: believe; Bible; 5 billion]

Did You Know?

The Eiffel Tower in Paris, France is _____ feet tall!

Can you guess how many pieces of steel were needed to build it? _____

Maurice Koechlin was the lead designer of the Eiffel Tower. He created over 5,000 drawings to help the construction workers know what to do.

He didn't make or put together any of the parts, but no one would deny he was the inspiration behind it all.

[answers: 1,063; 18,038 pieces of steel]

Lesson 1

Just like the Eiffel Tower, the Bible has many different writers but one designer, one inspiration behind it all, and that is God Himself.

The Bible is not a random collection of writings, it's God's message of love to the world!

> *John 14:6:*
> *Jesus told him, "I am the way, the truth and the life. No one comes to the Father except through me."*

Jesus says in John 14:6 that He is truth. So if Jesus and God are truth, then it makes sense that anything they create must be true!

Questions:

What is the Bible?

The Bible is a _____ of books printed together. Look at the index for all the names of the books.

"Bible" is from the Latin word _____, which means, "library" or "collection of books."

The Bible has _____ main sections: the Old Testament and the New Testament.

The _____ _____ is the larger of the two and includes everything from the creation of the world until just a few hundred years before Jesus.

The _____ _____ begins with the _____(the first four books), which are first-hand accounts of Jesus' life. The rest of the New Testament is how the early followers of Jesus were instructed to live and follow Jesus' teachings.

9

[answers: collection; biblia; two; Old Testament; New Testament; gospels]

Together the Bible was written over _____ years by at least _____ authors.

The Bible also has different types of literature: history, poetry, prophecy, and letters.

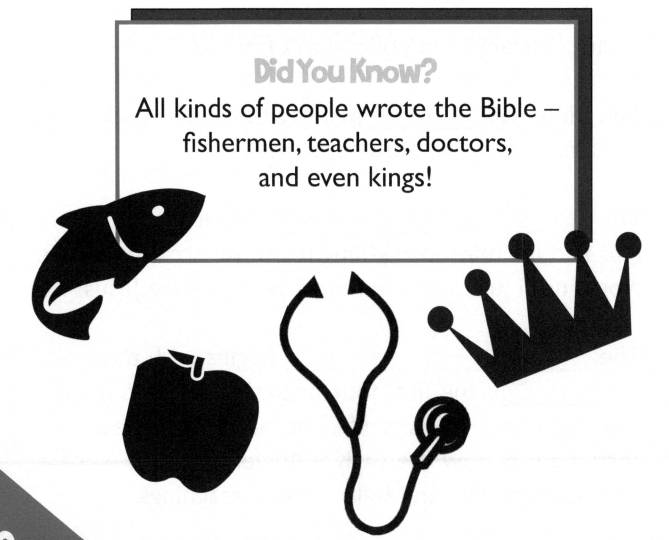

Did You Know?

All kinds of people wrote the Bible – fishermen, teachers, doctors, and even kings!

[answers: 1,600; 40]

The Bible

There are places in the world where it is illegal to do exactly what you are doing, holding a Bible. Some people risk their lives to get the Bible into the hands of people who aren't allowed to read it. Many people are killed for having a Bible.

Why do they risk their lives to read it? Why is it so precious to them?

It is precious to them because it is truth. The Bible is the answer. It is life. Just like Jesus, this book you hold in your hands is the way, the truth, and the life. There is nothing more precious.

Jesus summarized the entire Bible and all of God's instructions like this: "Love God and love others."

Journal:

What did you learn or discover about the Bible today?

What is your most precious possession? (Draw a picture or write about it.)

Journal:

What is one small goal you can set to make the Bible a bigger part of your life?

Write about what God is speaking to you this week.

We Believe For Kids!

Lesson 2

The Bible

Lesson 2

Big Question:

Why should the Bible matter to me?

What We Believe:

(Doctrinal Statement)

We believe the Bible is God's Word; it is truth. It serves as a trustworthy guide to our everyday lives.

Key Verse:

Write out the Key verse in the space below.

Hebrews 4:12

The Bible

Discussion Questions:
Get your pencils ready!

What do you think of when you hear the word "powerful"? Draw or describe something that is powerful.

What do you think of when you hear the word "personal"? Draw or describe something that is personal to you.

Lesson 2

Going Deeper:

(Hebrews 4:12; Ephesians 6:17; 2 Timothy 3:16)

The Bible is _____ and _____.

The Bible is a powerful _____ that we use to attack our enemy.

[answers: alive and powerful; weapon]

The Bible

According to Ephesians 6, who is our enemy?
(Ephesians 6:10-17)

What does it mean that
the Scriptures are "inspired"?
(2 Timothy 3:16)

Did You Know?
"Scripture"
is another name
for the Bible.

Lesson 2

Journal:

Journal:

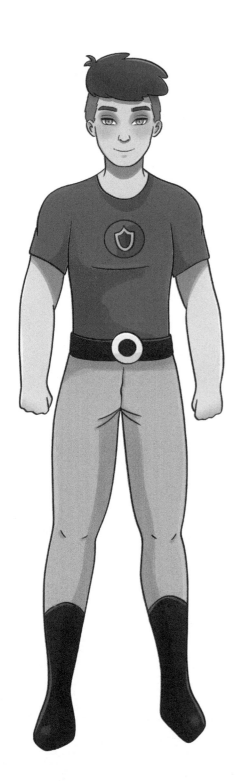

The Bible

Journal:

We Believe For Kids!

Lesson 3

The Bible

Lesson 3

Big Question:

How is the Bible useful for me today?

What We Believe:

(Doctrinal Statement)

We believe the Bible is God's Word; it is truth. It serves as a trustworthy guide to our everyday lives.

Key Verse:

Write out the key verse in the space below.

Psalm 119:105

The Bible

There are 66 books of the Bible,
which are divided into two sections:

Old Testament (39 books)

Genesis	1 Kings	Ecclesiastes	Obadiah
Exodus	2 Kings	Song of Solomon	Jonah
Leviticus	1 Chronicles	Isaiah	Micah
Numbers	2 Chronicles	Jeremiah	Nahum
Deuteronomy	Ezra	Lamentations	Habakkuk
Joshua	Nehemiah	Ezekiel	Zephaniah
Judges	Esther	Daniel	Haggai
Ruth	Job	Hosea	Zechariah
1 Samuel	Psalms	Joel	Malachi
2 Samuel	Proverbs	Amos	

New Testament (27 books)

Matthew	2 Corinthians	1 Timothy	2 Peter
Mark	Galatians	2 Timothy	1 John
Luke	Ephesians	Titus	2 John
John	Philippians	Philemon	3 John
Acts	Colossians	Hebrews	Jude
Romans	1 Thessalonians	James	Revelation
1 Corinthians	2 Thessalonians	1 Peter	

Going Deeper:

(Psalm 119:18; Jeremiah 33:3; John 14:26; 1 John 2:27)

The Bible is too hard to understand by ourselves. We need _____ to open our eyes to understand what we read.

Our spirit is the _____ part of our being. It's the part of us that holds our _____ and _____. It's the part that will remain alive after our body dies, the part that connects with God.

According to John 14:26 and 1 John 2:27, who is our helper when it comes to understanding the Bible?

[answers: God; nonphysical; emotions; character]

The Bible

Activation:

What are some strategies you think would help you read and understand the Bible?

What are the three strategies shared in your lesson today?

1. _____

2. _____

3. _____

NOTE: Journaling what you read and what God speaks to you through your reading is good to do no matter what strategy you use to read the Bible!

Lesson 3

There are several ways to journal:

- Draw/paint what you read

- Write out a letter from God to you that you feel He is telling you through your reading

- Use fancy calligraphy to write out your verse

- Use the SOAP method

The Bible

What is the SOAP method?

S: _____ - Write down the passage you read for the day.

O: _____ - What do you notice about the verse? Do you have questions?

A: _____ - How might this verse or story apply to your life or what you're going through today?

P: _____ - Ask God if there's anything else He wants you to know. Ask Him for help or tell Him you're sorry for ways you may have fallen short that came to your mind as you read.

[answers: Scripture; Observation; Application; Prayer]

Lesson 3

Journal:
Pick a verse and practice the SOAP method.

S:

O:

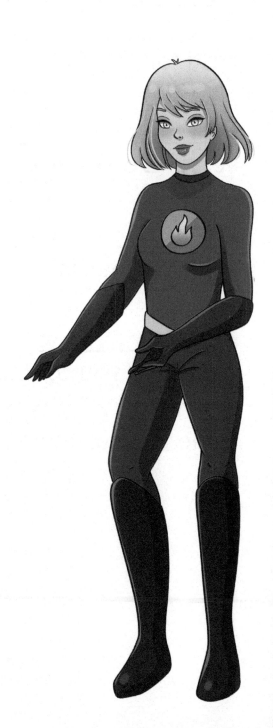

The Bible

Journal:

A:

P:

We Believe For Kids!

Lesson 4

Review

Lesson 4

Lessons to Review:

Take some time to review lessons 1, 2, and 3 in your journal, which cover The Bible.

Next, answer the following review questions and use your answers to complete the word search!

Review

Review Questions:

Fill in the blanks with words from the three lessons on the Bible. Then find the words in the puzzle.

1. _____ is something we believe that is based on what the Bible says.

2. The Bible is the _____-_____ book of the year, every year!

3. Christians believe that the Bible is 100% the creation of human authors but also 100% _____ by God.

4. The Bible is not a random collection of writings, it's God's message of _____ to the world!

5. The Bible is a _____ of books printed together.

6. "Bible" is from the Latin work "biblia," which means "_____" or "collection of books."

7. The Bible has two main sections: the _____ _____, which is the larger of the two and includes everything from the creation of the world until a few hundred years before Jesus; and the _____ _____, which includes firsthand accounts of Jesus and how the early followers of Jesus were instructed to live and follow his teachings.

8. The Bible is a _____ weapon that we use to attack our enemy (Satan).

9. The Bible was not just for people thousands of years ago, it is for you, it is _____.

10. The first four books of the New Testament are called the _____.

11. Our _____ is the nonphysical part of our being that holds our emotions and character. It is the part that connects with God.

12. The _____ _____ is our helper when it comes to understanding the Bible.

13. We talked about different methods for studying the Bible, including the SOAP method. SOAP stands for _____, _____, _____, _____.

14. The doctrinal statement for these last few weeks states that, "We believe the Bible is God's Word; it is _____. It serves as a _____ guide to our everyday lives.

Lesson 4

Word Search:

```
Q L B F S F E V Z V C S D B B X C E Q Y H V U H L
Q L F S G T X P E M O C P S J E I A A L K L U F F
H X U C J J V L U R R D U S K H S O L S Q H B F P
N T X I W X N V X F R G Q R E B F T X R Z D T P U
B R I Q K F M D I G F M H W G R P S S Q V A K L L
V U T C Q Y B G U T B C S Z T D I N I E G N X Y C
K S F P N Y E J G O S P E L S F Z S S T L M P E D
S T H G U E X Q U S P I R I T P R A Y E R L A J H
K W K L I B R A R Y P V G S H A H U M Z J B I R H
W O C R R P A S J K X Y E D V H P K S R F I W N W
J R N L K O L D T E S T A M E N T E L V H I Q A G
O T Q L M Z T B A P H H N Q H G H A P P N C E S H
B H X O I H M C G A X C V H B M H H K V C D N X R
S Y U V S C R I P T U R E E E G Z C Q Z K Z J L J
E P T E X N J M E C J C N E W T E S T A M E N T B
R Q P X G M V A S I C R Q W F T Z T T R U T H R I
V N C J B E N E J W Q Z D V D H R Y I V Y C O G R
A S H P E R S O N A L T R A G A H V N Q P K X I N
T W Q R F E I X P O W E R F U L Y Y S O J H D G O
I L D O C T R I N E K G X P X W M X P Q L V E R A
O U T X C O L L E C T I O N M Y Q X I Z Y T O J N
N X C T W E P O T C N L T A W K L I R E B K X X E
R Z C C E A P C R Q I F Z I X P C P E T I C G C C
M U X H O L Y S P I R I T X N M V A D S D J J W Y
A S N Y R D T H P W D M A P P L I C A T I O N P I
```

Review

Answers:

Old Testament

New Testament

trustworthy

best-selling

application

collection

Holy Spirit

observation

Scripture

doctrine

powerful

personal

gospels

inspired

library

prayer

truth

Spirit

love

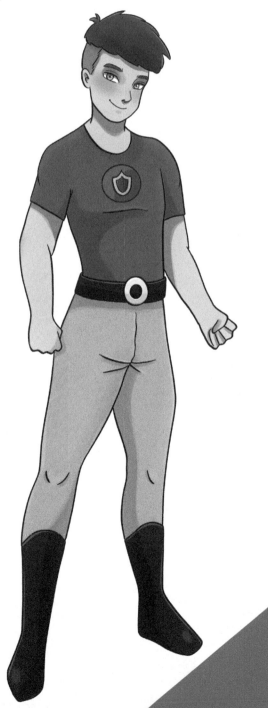

We Believe For Kids!

Lesson 5

God the Father

Lesson 5

Big Question:

Who/what is God?

What We Believe:
(Doctrinal Statement)

We believe God is the eternal, all-powerful, all-knowing, everywhere-present, and unchangeable Creator of all, who is also the God of love, mercy, and compassion.

Key Verse:

Write out the key verse in the space below.

1 John 3:1

God the Father

Going Deeper:

According to Deuteronomy 6:4, there is only ONE GOD, but Matthew 28:19 tells us that He shows Himself to us as three persons united in one Godhead. He has shown Himself as a:

• _____ - the Creator of all things
  (Genesis 1:1)

• _____ - Jesus, Savior of the whole world
  (John 3:16)

• _____ - the Holy Spirit, who lives in us and guides us to do what is right
  (John 14:17, 26)

This week we are talking about God as our _____ Father.

[answers: Father; Son; Helper; Heavenly]

Lesson 5

Questions:

What can we do to know our Heavenly Father better?

Did You Know?

God cares for us so much that He knows the number of hairs on our heads!
(Matthew 10:30-31)
Take a small chunk of hair and see if you can count how many hairs are in that small chunk! It's hard!

Questions: (cont.)

We are made in God's image, so we share some of his attributes or qualities. Can you name some below?

There are also attributes or qualities that are unique to only God.

- God is a _____. We cannot see Him with our natural eyes *(John 1:18; John 4:24; Hebrews 11:3)*.

- What are some examples of other things you know exist even though you can't see them?

[answers: spirit]

Questions: (cont.)

- God is _____. He is all-powerful
  (Isaiah 40:28-31).

- What is the hardest task in the whole world?
  God can do it. Never be afraid to ask Him for
  help. Nothing is too big (or too small) for Him.
  What is something you are asking God for help
  with?

Questions: (cont.)

- God is _____. He knows everything. He knows all you have done and all that has been done to you *(Psalms 139:1-6)*.

  If you are not sure about something, just ask Him about it and He will make it clearer for you.

- God is _____. He is everywhere *(Psalms 139:7-12; Matthew 28:20; Hebrews 13: 5)*. Wherever you are, God is with you.

  There is no need to feel alone or afraid. He will never leave you or forsake you.

- God is _____. He cannot tolerate sin *(1 Peter 1:16)*.

[answers: omniscient, omnipresent, holy]

Lesson 5

Questions: (cont.)

What does sin do to our relationship with God?

God the Father

Activation:

If you keep flinging paint at a canvas, do you think you will ever produce an image as clear as this picture?

When you see the Mona Lisa, do you think, "What a happy accident?" or do you think, "Wow, an artist must have painted and created this work of art?"

Did You Know?

"Mona Lisa" was not her name.

The painting is smaller than you might think. It is only 8 inches longer and 4 inches wider than this workbook opened up flat.

Lesson 5

Journal:

How are we like God? How are we different from God?

Did you learn something about God in this lesson that surprised you? If so, what?

Journal:

How does it make you feel to know that God knows what you are doing every minute of the day?

Were you surprised to learn that God wants a relationship with you?

Activity

Draw a line from each characteristic that we share with God to the figure of the person and draw a line from each characteristic that is unique to God to the word "God".

Goodness
Merciful
Eternal
Infinite
Loving
Gentle
Omniscient (all-knowing)
Peaceful
Kind
Just
Patient
Sovereign (supreme authority)

GOD

We Believe For Kids!

Lesson 6

God the Son

Lesson 6

Big Question:

Who is Jesus Christ?

What We Believe:
(Doctrinal Statement)

We believe Jesus is co-Creator with the Father. Conceived miraculously, He is all human and all God. He died and rose again to make possible our relationship with God. Now He is in heaven with the Father praying for us.

Key Verse:

Write out the Key verse in the space below.

Romans 5:8

Going Deeper:

According to Matthew 1:18, who was Jesus' mother? _____. Who was his father? _____.

Who is "the Word"? *(John 1:1; John 1:14)*

_____

God and Jesus are the same person fulfilling different roles (John 14:9-10). What are some of the different roles that you have in your life?
(Example: son, daughter, student...)

[answers: Mary; God (Holy Spirit); Jesus]

Jesus becoming _____ enabled us to see what God was like; it helped us to relate to Him.

Jesus became the perfect _____ _____ for how we should act.

God's plan is to give us a hopeful future, a future we can look forward to *(Jeremiah 29:11)*.

Nonetheless because of Adam and Eve's disobedience toward God in the Garden of Eden, we all are born with a sin nature, our natural desire to do what is wrong *(Romans 3:23)*.

God's original plan was to have a close relationship with us. He made us in his image and gave us power over all things, but Adam and Eve's sin created a distance between us and God. In other words, sin separated us from God.

[answers: human; role model]

God the Son

God wanted to remove the distance between us, but there was a costly price that needed to be paid. The Bible says that the wages (payment) for sin is death (Romans 6:23). Because of our sin, we are sentenced to not just a physical death, but also a spiritual death where we are separated from God forever.

God looked everywhere to find a perfect person who had not sinned so that he or she could pay the price for everyone by dying, even though he or she didn't deserve to die. He couldn't find even one person, so He sent his only Son to earth in human form to pay the price for us. Jesus Christ, God's Son, was crucified on a cross for our sins. He then defeated sin and death by raising from the dead and ascending back to heaven.

When we accept Jesus as our Savior, we can conquer the sin that separates us from God and have a relationship with our Heavenly Father, through his Son, Jesus Christ (John 3:16).

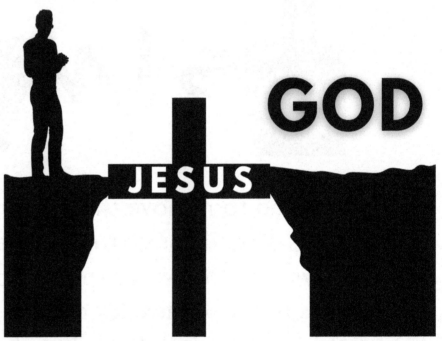

Did You Know?

After we accept Jesus as our Savior, when God sees us, He sees the righteousness (right standing) of his Son Jesus - not our sin!

Activation:

Activity 1
Unscramble the verse below:

JESSU EVAG SHI ILFE FRO URO SNIS, TUSJ SA DGO
URO HERTAF PLNNAED, NI RDERO OT ESRUEC
SU MROF ISHT LIVE WLDOR NI WCIHH EW ILVE.

J __ __ __ __   __ __ __ __   __ __ __   __ __
__ __   __ __ __   __ __ __
__ __ __ __, __ __ __ __   __ __   __ __ __
O __ __   F __ __ __ __ __
__ __ __ __ __ __ __, __ __   __ __ __ __ __
__ __   __ __ __ __ __   __ __
__ __ __ __   __ __ __ __   __ __ __ __   __ __
__ __ __   __ __   __ __ __ __ __
__ __   __ __ __ __.

Questions:

Do you believe in Jesus Christ? Why or why not?

Do you believe that He died on the cross for your sins and rose again?

Have you asked Him to forgive you for the wrong things you have done? Are you willing to turn away from doing what is wrong?

God the Son

If you would like to ask Jesus to forgive your sins and be your Savior, ask your teacher or another trusted adult to lead you in prayer. Or you can pray the following prayer (or one like it) in your heart and ask Jesus to forgive you and help you to have a relationship with Him.

Dear Heavenly Father,

You paid a huge price for my sins by sending your Son to die on the cross for me. Thank you for doing that! When I think about my life, I realize that I have done things and thought about things that are wrong, and I am sorry. Please forgive me. Please replace my sinful nature, my desire to do and think wrong things, with your nature, with your Holy Spirit instead. Help me to do the things that make You happy.

In Jesus' name I pray, amen.

Lesson 6

If you prayed a prayer to begin your new relationship with Jesus, make sure to tell your teacher or parents! Each time one of us begins a new relationship with Jesus, there is a party in heaven! So let people in your life celebrate with you and the angels!

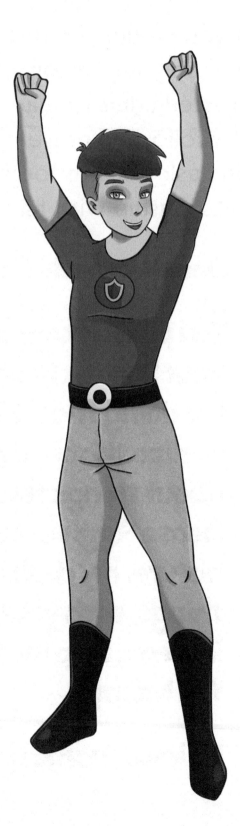

We Believe For Kids!

Lesson 7

God the
Holy Spirit

Lesson 7

Big Question:

Who is the Holy Spirit?

What We Believe:
(Doctrinal Statement)

We believe in God the Holy Spirit, co-Creator with the Father and the Son. He helps us know when we've done wrong, make good decisions, and learn what is true. He gives us power and the tools to be like Jesus.

Key Verse:

Write out the Key verse in the space below.

John 14:16

God the Holy Spirit

Questions:

According to John 14:16, the Holy Spirit is our

_____.

When you hear the word "helper," what comes to mind?

Going Deeper:

Romans 8:11

The Spirit of God, who raised Jesus from the dead, lives in you. And just as God raised Christ Jesus from the dead, he will give life to your mortal bodies by this same Spirit living within you.

If God's Spirit lives inside of you, should you be afraid? _____!

Did You Know?

That weird feeling we get when we are doing something wrong is the Holy Spirit's way of showing us that what we are doing is not right.

[answers: No!]

God the Holy Spirit

What are ways the Holy Spirit helps us?

- The Holy Spirit _____ for us
  (Romans 8:26).

- The Holy Spirit helps us to _____
  _____ *(Colossians 1:8)*.

- The Holy Spirit helps us to _____
  _____ better *(Ephesians 1:17)*.

The Bible states that the Holy Spirit produces good qualities, or "fruit," in our lives: love, joy, peace, patience, kindness, goodness, faithfulness, gentleness, and self-control *(Galatians 5:22-23)*.

[answers: Prays; love others; understand God]

Activation:

Fill in the blanks with the following words:

Guide	Helper	Prays	Teaches	Us
God	Power	Of the Spirit	Jesus	God

The Holy Spirit is our _____. The Holy Spirit was sent by _____.

He is also fully _____ and he lives inside of _____.

The Holy Spirit give us _____ so we should not be afraid. The Holy Spirit _____ for us.

He also makes us more like _____. He helps us to develop the fruits _____ _____ _____.

The Holy Spirit _____ us what to say.

We should allow the Holy Spirit to _____ us.

We Believe For Kids!

Lesson 8

Review

Lesson 8

Lessons to Review:

Take some time to review lessons 5, 6, and 7 in your journal, which cover God the Father, God the Son, and God the Holy Spirit.

Next, answer the following review questions and use your answers to complete the crossword puzzle!

Review

Review Questions:

Fill in the blanks with words from the three lessons on God. Then find the words in the puzzle.

1. God shows Himself to us as _____ persons united in one Godhead *(Matthew 28:19)*.

2. The three persons of the Godhead are: God the _____, God the _____, and God the Holy _____.

3. We are made in God's image, so we share some of his attributes or qualities. Which of the following do we share with God?
   a. omnipotence, omniscience, omnipresence, holiness
   b. goodness, mercy, love
   c. eyes, legs, hands

4. _____ means that God is all powerful.

5. _____ means that God is all knowing.

6. _____ means that God is everywhere.

7. Since Jesus was born to an earthly mother, he is fully _____.

8. Since Jesus was born to a Heavenly Father, he is fully _____.

9. We can know what the Father is like by knowing _____ (the Son).

10. Our natural desire to do what is wrong is called a _____ nature.

11. Our sin _____ us from God.

12. By his death and resurrection, Jesus paid the _____ for our sin.

13. The Holy Spirit is our _____.

14. The Holy Spirit does which of the following for us:

    a. Works in our hearts to make us better children of God

    b. Tries to prevent us from doing what is wrong

    c. Prays for us

    d. Helps us to love others

    e. Helps us to understand God better

    f. All of the above

15. The Holy Spirit produces good "_____" in our lives: love, joy, peace, patience, kindness, goodness, faithfulness, gentleness, and self-control *(Galatians 5:22-23)*.

Crossword:

Review

Crossword Answers:

Down:

1. the Holy Spirit acts as this to us

2. all powerful

3. the Holy Spirit produces this in us

4. everywhere

5. part of the Godhead

7. what our sin does between us and God

10. born of an earthly mother

12. born of a Heavenly Father

13. natural desire to do wrong

15. part of the Godhead

Across:

6. the Son

8. paid for by Jesus

9. part of the Godhead

11. number of persons united in one Godhead

14. all knowing

We Believe For Kids!

Lesson 9

God
Speaks

Big Question:

How does God communicate with us?

What We Believe:
(Doctrinal Statement)

We believe that even though God is the eternal, all-powerful, all-knowing, everywhere-present, and un-changeable Creator of all, He wants a relationship with each one of us.

Key Verse:

Write out the Key verse in the space below.

John 10:27

God Speaks

Questions:

What do healthy friendships look like? Write or draw about them in the space below.

What are some ways that God speaks to people today?

Lesson 9

Many key people in the Bible began hearing from God when they were your age! God doesn't just speak to adults; He also speaks to kids.

Jesus told his disciples that his entire kingdom belongs to kids (Luke 18:16), so there is nothing in his kingdom that doesn't include you. His gifts, his voice, his Word, his Holy Spirit – God wants you to experience all of it!

God Speaks

Going Deeper:

Read these passages and write down the ways God spoke to these young people:

- **Samuel** *(Samuel 3:1-10)*

- **David** *(Psalm 40:3)*

- **Joseph** *(Genesis 37:5-11)*

- **Daniel** *(Daniel 7:1)*

- **Mary** *(Luke 1:26)*

Did You Know?

Even though its ears are extremely simple, a moth can sense frequencies up to 300 kilohertz, well beyond the range of any other animal and higher than any bat can squeak.

God Speaks

Did You Know?

Elephants have some of the best hearing around. They can hear at frequencies 20 times lower than humans. It isn't just their ears that perceive sound; these majestic beasts also have receptors in their trunks and feet that are excellent at picking up low-frequency vibrations.

The Bible shows us that God not only spoke to adults but to kids as well. But what about now? Does He still speak to us today?

Lesson 9

John 8:47:
Anyone who belongs to God listens gladly to the words of God.

John 10:27:
My sheep listen to my voice; I know them, and they follow me.

Jeremiah 33:3:
Ask me and I will tell you remarkable secrets you do not know about things to come.

Deuteronomy 30:14:
No, the message is very close at hand; it is on your lips and in your heart so that you can obey it.

God Speaks

There are two voices other than God's voice that fight for our attention. Whose are they?

Fill in the blanks below and then write some of the ways we can recognize these voices.

_____'s Voice:

_____ _____ Voice:

Activation:

God's Voice

What is God speaking to you right now?

God Speaks

My Voice

What are some of the things you tell yourself often?

These might be positive or negative. How do you feel about yourself? How do you feel about your life, your family, your friends? What are some of your core wants and desires you think about often?

Satan's Voice

What do you suspect Satan says to you?

What are some major fears you struggle with, ugly feelings you have toward yourself or others, or lies he may be trying to tell you?

God Speaks

Journal:

Have you ever heard from God before? Write about it. Remind yourself of a time you felt God was speaking to you about something.

Lesson 9

Journal:

If there is one way you'd love to start hearing from God, which way would it be? Pray for God to begin speaking to you in that way, and expect to receive that gift! He wants you to hear Him even more than you want it.

God Speaks

Journal:

Practice listening to God by asking Him a question and sitting quietly until you hear or feel Him answer. Example: "God, how do you feel about me?" Or, "God, what kind of a day am I going to have today?" Journal whatever you hear, and remember to pay attention to whether it has the characteristics of God's words, your words, or Satan's words.

We Believe For Kids!

Lesson 10

Worldview

Lesson 10

Big Question:

Isn't all truth equal? Who are you to say that your "truth" is right?

What We Believe:
(Doctrinal Statement)

We believe the Bible is God's Word; it is truth. It serves as a trustworthy guide to our everyday lives.

Key Verse:

Write out the key verse in the space below.

John 8:32

Worldview

Questions:

The term "doctrine" simply means a set of beliefs held and taught by a church, political party, or other group.

Why do you think it is so important to take this class, to study "doctrine"?

What is a "worldview"?

Lesson 10

Five Worldviews:

Naturalism— Atheism; Agnosticism; Existentialism

Reality - The material universe (what we can see, hear, taste, smell, or touch) is all that exists. There are no such things as souls or spirits. Everything is explained by natural law.

Man - Humans are simply a product of evolution. When we die, we cease to exist. All humankind will one day cease to exist.

Truth - Truth is that which can be explained through science. It is what we can explain through our five senses.

Values - No objective values or morals exist. Morals are individual preferences or socially useful behaviors, subject to change.

Worldview

Pantheism— Hinduism; Taoism; Buddhism; New Age

Reality - Only the spiritual dimension exists. Everything we can see, hear, taste, smell, or touch is just an illusion. Spiritual reality is eternal, impersonal, and unknowable. Everything is a part of "God," or "God" is in everything and everyone.

Man - Humans are one with ultimate reality (God). Therefore we are spiritual, eternal, and impersonal. Our belief that we are individuals is just an illusion.

Truth - Truth is an experience of unity with the "oneness" of the universe. Truth is beyond all rational description. Rational thought as we understand it cannot show us reality.

Values - Many pantheistic thinkers believe there is no real distinction between good and evil. Instead, "unenlightened" behavior is that which fails to understand the unity between us, others, and God.

Lesson 10

Reality - An infinite, personal God exists. He created a finite, material world. Reality is both material (what you can see, hear, taste, smell, or touch) and spiritual. The universe as we know it had a beginning and will have an end, but there is an afterlife (life after the life we experience on this earth).

Man - Humans are the unique creation of God. People were created "in the image of God," which means that we are personal, eternal, spiritual, and physical.

Truth - God reveals the truth about Himself (revelation). Truth about the material world is gained by revelation and the five senses in conjuntion with rational thought.

Values - Our moral values are the expression of an absolute moral being.

Worldview

Spiritism & Polytheism -

Reality - The world is filled with spirit beings who govern what goes on. Gods and demons are the real reason behind "natural" events. Material things are real, but they have spirits associated with them, and therefore, can be interpreted spiritually.

Man - Humans, like the rest of the creatures on earth, are created by the gods. Often, tribes or races have a special relationship with some gods whom they feel protect them and can punish them.

Truth - Truth about the natural world is discovered through a "shaman," or special, spiritual figure. These figures experience visions telling them what the gods and demons are doing and how they feel.

Values - Moral values take the form of taboos, which are things that irritate or anger various spirits. The "taboos" are different from the idea of "good and evil" because they feel it is just as important to avoid irritating evil spirits as it is good ones.

Lesson 10

Postmodernism –

Reality – Reality must be interpreted through our language and cultural "paradigm," or our own framework of experiences.

Man – Humans are a product of their cultural reality or social setting. The idea that people are autonomous (free to govern themselves, able to control their own behavior) is a myth.

Truth – We are free to decide our own truths. Our truth may not apply to other cultural settings. Truth is relative to one's culture. There is no such thing as "absolute truth."

Values – Values are also part of our social and cultural "paradigms," or settings. Tolerance, freedom of expression, inclusion, and refusal to claim to have the truth are the only universal values.

Worldview

Going Deeper:

Which of these worldviews do you agree with more than others?

Lesson 10

Philippians 2:7-8:
You must have the same attitude that Christ Jesus had. Though he was God he did not think of equality with God as something to cling to. Instead, he gave up his divine privileges; he took the humble position of a slave and was born as a human being. When he appeared in human form, he humbled himself in obedience to God and died a criminal's death on a cross.

How did Jesus' worldview affect others?

How could your worldview affect others?

Philippines 2:9-11:
Therefore, God elevated him to the place of highest honor and gave him the name above all other names, that at the name of Jesus every knee should bow, in heaven and on earth and under the earth, and every tongue declare that Jesus Christ is Lord, to the glory of God the Father.

Journal:

Do you agree with the statement that all truths are equal, or that truth is subjective (whatever we want it to be)? Do you believe it is fine to believe whatever you want to believe? Why or why not?

Lesson 10

Journal:

Have you ever thought about your own world-view? Has it changed since taking this class?

Journal:

Describe your own worldview using your own words. It is good to know what you believe and why you believe it.

We Believe For Kids!

Lesson 11

Book
Review

Lessons to Review:

Take some time to review all of the lessons that you have covered in this class.

You can use the following **"Main Points"** to help in your review.

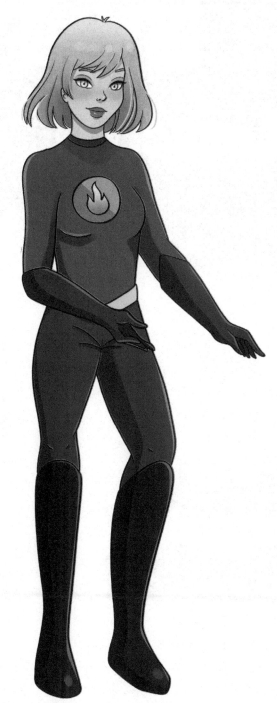

Book Review

Review Lessons 1-3: The Bible

Doctrinal Statement:

We believe the Bible is God's Word; it is truth. It serves as a trustworthy guide to our everyday lives.

Key Verses:

2 Timothy 3:16:
All Scripture is inspired by God and is useful to teach us what is true and to make us realize what is wrong in our lives. It corrects us when we are wrong and teaches us to do what is right.

Hebrews 4:12:
For the word of God is alive and powerful. It is sharper than the sharpest two-edged sword, cutting between soul and spirit, between joint and marrow. It exposes our innermost thoughts and desires.

Psalm 119:105:
Your word is a lamp to guide my feet and a light for my path.

Lesson 11

Main Points:

- The Bible is 100 percent the creation of human authors but also 100 percent inspired by God. God himself breathed this Truth into existence. He planted the words in the minds of many writers, helping them create this book that is capable of guiding us when we are lost, revealing God's love for us and transforming our lives.

- There are two main sections: the **Old Testament** and the **New Testament**. The Old Testament is the larger of the two testaments and includes everything from the creation of the world until just a few hundred years before Jesus. The first four books of the New Testament are called the gospels. They are firsthand accounts of the life of Jesus. The rest of the New Testament recounts how the early followers of Jesus were instructed to live and follow Jesus' teachings.

- The Bible was written over a time span of **1,600 years** by at least **40 authors**, which included kings, scholars, tax collectors, philosophers, fishermen, statesmen, poets, historians, teachers, prophets, and doctors.

- The Bible contains different types of literature: **history**, **poetry**, **prophecy**, and even letters. More than **300 prophetic details** (details mentioned before they actually happened) about Jesus' life found in the Old Testament came true, such as the fact that He would be born of a virgin, his birthplace would be Bethlehem, and that He would be crucified between two thieves.

- **The Bible is powerful.** God's Word is our main weapon for battle. It's part of the armor of God (Ephesians 6:17).

- "**Scripture**" is another word for "**Bible**." Scripture is inspired or "**God-breathed.**"

- When God sent Jesus to us, it was another way for Him to send his very words to us. When Jesus spoke, He spoke God's words. When we read the Bible, we read God's words.

Lesson 11

- **The Bible is personal.** If you want to know who God made you to be or what He thinks of you, this is the only book you need.

- **The Bible isn't something our brain can understand all by itself.** It was written not just for our brain, but also for our spirit. The most powerful thing you can do to help yourself understand God's Word is to invite the Holy Spirit to read it with you.

- **Our spirit is the nonphysical part of our being.** It's the part of us that holds our emotions and character. It's the part that will remain alive after our body dies, the part that connects to God.

- **There are so many great ways to read the Bible.** Lesson 3 gave you three ideas: reading plans or devotionals, reading one book of the Bible at a time, or asking the Holy Spirit to guide you to a passage.

- Regardless of what method you choose, there is one thing that is so important: **Journal what you read** and what God speaks to you through your reading.

One popular way to journal is the **SOAP** method:

Scripture - Write down the Scripture passage you read.

Observation - What do you notice about the verse? Do you have questions?

Application - How might this verse or story apply to your life or what you're going through today?

Pray - Ask God if there's anything else He wants you to know and write down anything you hear Him saying.

Review Lessons 5-7:
God the Father; God the Son; God the Holy Spirit

Doctrinal Statements:

We believe God is the eternal, all-powerful, all-knowing, everywhere-present, and unchangeable Creator of all, who is also the God of love, mercy, and compassion.

We believe Jesus is co-Creator with the Father. Conceived miraculously, He is all human and all God. He died and rose again to make possible our relationship with God. Now He is in heaven with the Father praying for us.

We believe in God the Holy Spirit, co-Creator with the Father and the Son. He helps us know when we've done wrong, make good decisions, and learn what is true. He gives us power and the tools to be like Jesus.

Book Review

Key Verses:

1 John 3:1:
See how very much our Father loves us, for he calls us his children, and that is what we are! But the people who belong to this world don't recognize that we are God's children because they don't know him.

Romans 5:8:
But God showed his great love for us by sending Christ to die for us while we were still sinners.

John 14:16:
And I will ask the Father, and he will give you another Advocate, who will never leave you.

Main Points:

* **There is only one God**, but He shows himself to us as three persons united in one Godhead (Matthew 28:19). **God the Father**, **God the Son**, and **God the Holy Spirit**.

Lesson 11

- **We are God's children** (Romans 8:16). We are God's creation, created for his purpose. God made us for a reason; we were not created by chance (Isaiah 64:8). We are special.

- **We are made in God's image**, so we share some of his attributes or qualities. Examples: goodness, mercy, and love.

- There are some qualities that are unique to God alone. God is a spirit. God is omnipotent (Isaiah 40:28-31). God is omniscient (Psalms 139:1-6). God is omnipresent (Psalms 139:7-12). God is holy (1 Peter 1:16).

- **Jesus was born to an earthly mother**, which makes Him fully human and **He was born to a Heavenly Father**, which makes Him fully God. Jesus told us in Scripture that He and the Father are the same. They are the same person fulfilling different roles (John 14:9-10).

Book Review

- **God and his Word cannot be separated;** they are one and the same. So, to say the Word became flesh and made his home among us is to say God himself came in human form to live with us (John 1:1; 1:14).

- Jesus becoming human enabled us to see what God is like; it helped us to relate to Him.

- **A sin nature,** our natural desire to do what is wrong, was passed down from Adam and Eve into all humans born thereafter (Romans 3:23). This was not what God intended. God's original plan was to have a close relationship with us. He made us in his image and gave us power over all things, but **Adam and Eve's sin separated us from God.**

- God wanted to bring us back to Him, but there was a price that had to be paid. The Bible states that **the wages for sin is death** (Romans 6:23).

- God looked everywhere but **there was no one who was sinless** – not one person (Psalm 53:2-3; Romans 3:10-12).

Lesson 11

- **Jesus Christ, God's Son, was crucified** on the cross **for our sins**. Christ later rose from the dead and ascended to heaven. **He defeated sin and death**, and removed the distance between people and God. Now **we can have a relationship with God** our Father **through his Son, Jesus Christ**.

- **Everyone who believes in Jesus Christ**, who died on the cross for our sins and rose from the dead, **shall be saved**. But first we need to **ask God to forgive us** for all the wrong things we have done and turn away from doing wrong.

- Now, when God, our Heavenly Father, sees us He sees the righteousness of his Son, Jesus Christ. This means that **we are now in right standing with God but only through Jesus Christ**.

- When we accept Jesus Christ as our Savior, his Spirit comes and lives inside our hearts. His Spirit is our Helper.

Book Review

- **The Holy Spirit was sent by God** to carry out his will in and through us. He is at work in our hearts to make us better children of God. He tries to prevent us from doing what is wrong. He prays for us and helps us with our weaknesses (Romans 8:26). The Holy Spirit helps us to love others (Colossians 1:8) and to understand God better (Ephesians 1:17).

- **We can relate to the Holy Spirit as a person**, not a thing, because the Holy Spirit can teach, pray, love, and feel sadness just as we do (Isaiah 63:10).

- The Bible states that the **Holy Spirit produces good qualities, or "fruit," in our lives**: love, joy, peace, patience, kindness, goodness, faithfulness, gentleness, and self-control (Galatians 5:22-23).

Review Lessons 9-10:
God Speaks; Worldview

Doctrinal Statements:

We believe that even though God is the eternal, all-powerful, all-knowing, everywhere-present, and unchangeable Creator of all, He wants a relationship with each one of us.

We believe the Bible is God's Word; it is truth. It serves as a trustworthy guide to our everyday lives.

Key Verses:

John 10:27:
My sheep listen to my voice; I know them, and they follow me.

John 8:32:
And you will know the truth, and the truth will set you free.

Book Review

Main Points:

- **God doesn't just speak to adults; He also speaks to kids.** Jesus told his disciples that his entire kingdom belongs to kids (Luke 18:16), so there's nothing in his kingdom that doesn't include you. His gifts, his voice, his Word, his Holy Spirit — **God wants you to experience all of it!**

- Examples of people in the Bible hearing from God: Samuel (1 Samuel 3:1-10); David (Psalm 40:3); Joseph (Genesis 37:5-11); Daniel (Daniel 7:1); Mary (Luke 1: 26, 46-55). God spoke not only to adults but to kids, and **He not only spoke to people in the Bible, He speaks to us today!** (John 8:47; John 10:27; Jeremiah 33:3; Deuteronomy 30:14).

- **God's words are living and active.** They are powerful, transformative, sweet, perfect, true, enlightening, helpful, kind, and lovely.

- If we don't feel better or cleaner or more free after hearing something, it's not God. Even his corrections are sweet and lead us toward freedom and joy. **He will never lie to you,** or be cruel to you, or hurt you in any way.

- It is challenging to learn how to tell the difference between God's voice and other voices that influence our lives. **The three most common voices we hear are: God's voice, Satan's voice, and our own voice.**

- **Satan is our enemy.** Scripture says he's a deceiver and an accuser, so when he speaks **he will try to lie, trick, confuse, anger, blame, or scare you.** If you're hearing something that makes you feel those emotions, it's often Satan who is behind it.

- Our voice speaks to us about our own wants and desires. It's interested in our comfort and is pretty self-serving. **If our thoughts are consumed with what's best for us** and what we want or wish, odds are **it's our own voice** speaking to us.

  - The term "doctrine" simply means a set of beliefs held and taught by a church, political party, or other group.

- **Worldview is how we think about the world.** It's a collection of attitudes, values, and expectations about the world around us. **Your worldview influences your every thought and action.** It affects your choices, how you act in certain situations. It determines how you spend your time and your money. It even helps determine what you decide to do with your life.

- Five Worldviews: **Naturalism** (Atheism; Agnosticism; Existentialism); **Pantheism** (Hinduism; Taoism; Buddhism; New Age); **Theism** (Christianity; Islam; Judaisim); **Spiritism** & **Polytheism**; Postmodernism.

- **Naturalism** (Atheism; Agnosticism; Existentialism) - The material universe (what we can see, hear, taste, smell, or touch) is all that exists. There are no such things as souls or spirits. Everything is explained by natural law. Humans are simply a product of evolution. When we die, we cease to exist. All humankind will one day cease to exist.

Lesson 11

Truth is that which can be explained through science. It is what we can explain through our five senses. No objective values or morals exist. Morals are individual preferences or socially useful behaviors, subject to change.

- **Pantheism** (Hinduism; Taoism; Buddhism; New Age) - Only the spiritual dimension exists. Everything we can see, hear, taste, smell, or touch is just an illusion. Spiritual reality is eternal, impersonal, and unknowable. Everything is a part of "God," or "God" is in everything and everyone. Humans are one with ultimate reality (God). Therefore we are spiritual, eternal, and impersonal. Our belief that we are individuals is just an illusion. Truth is an experience of unity with the "oneness" of the universe. Truth is beyond all rational description. Rational thought as we understand it cannot show us reality. Many pantheistic thinkers believe there is no real distiniction between good and evil. Instead, "unenlightened" behavior is that which fails to understand the unity between us, others, and God.

- **Theism** (Christianity; Islam; Judaisim) - An infinite, personal God exists. He created a finite, material world. Reality is both material (what you can see, hear, taste, smell, or touch) and spiritual. The universe as we know it had a beginning and will have an end, but there is an afterlife (life after the life we experience on this earth). Humans are the unique creation of God. People were created "in the image of God," which means that we are personal, eternal, spiritual, and physical. God reveals the truth about Himself (revelation). Truth about the material world is gained by revelation and the five senses in conjuntion with rational thought.Our moral values are the expression of an absolute moral being.

- **Spiritism & Polytheism** - The world is filled with spirit beings who govern what goes on. Gods and demons are the real reason behind "natural" events. Material things are real, but they have spirits associated with them, and therefore, can be interpreted spiritually. Humans, like the rest of the creatures on earth, are created by the gods. Often, tribes or races have a special relationship with some gods whom they feel protect them and can punish them. Truth about the natural world is discovered through a "shaman," or special, spiritual figure. These figures experience visions telling them what the gods and demons are doing and how they feel. Moral values take the form of taboos, which are things that irritate or anger various spirits. The "taboos" are different from the idea of "good and evil" because they feel it is just as important to avoid irritating evil spirits as it is good ones.

- **Postmodernism** - Reality must be interpreted through our language and cultural "paradigm," or our own framework of experiences. Humans are a product of their cultural reality or social setting. The idea that people are autonomous (free to govern themselves, able to control their own behavior) is a myth. We are free to decide our own truths. Our truth may not apply to other cultural settings. Truth is relative to one's culture. There is no such thing as "absolute truth." Values are also part of our social and cultural "paradigms," or settings. Tolerance, freedom of expression, inclusion, and refusal to claim to have the truth are the only universal values.

- If truth is subjective, you should be able to believe whatever you want, but what about things like believing your doctor's diagnosis and treatment options? Or people that drive under the influence of drugs or alcohol because they "believe" they are fine?

- It's even more important to know spiritual truth.

- A follower of Christ's worldview relies on the fact that God's Word is truth, just as we learned in Lessons 1 through 3. The Bible is the Word of God; it is truth. The fact that the Word of God is truth was Jesus' worldview, and He acted on that belief.

- **Jesus' worldview affected us because it provides us with salvation when we accept Him as**

our Savior. Our worldview can affect others because we can either point people to Jesus or away from him.

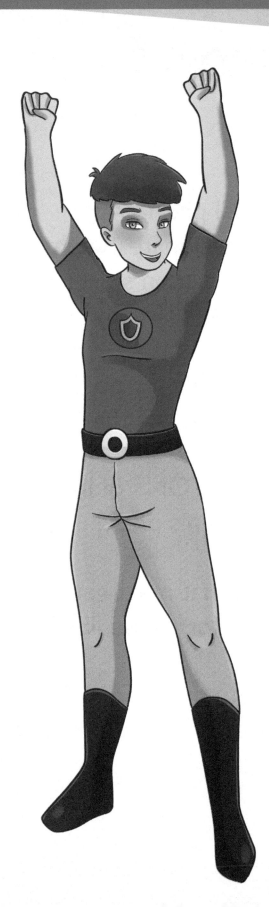

Appendix

Skit-Lesson 1

Two characters: **Ralph and Abby**

[Abby finds Ralph typing on his cell phone. Abby is wise, knowledgeable, and compassionate. Ralph finishes sending a post of some kind, then starts a conversation about getting some likes already.]

Ralph: Hey Abby, are you going to like my post? I mean, how many dogs can skateboard like that?

Abby: That is pretty cool. You'll get TONS of likes! [Abby pulls out her phone and likes his post.]

[Transition] **Abby:** Another thing that must get a lot of likes is a book I've been waiting for at the library. It has a really long waiting list.

Ralph: I usually wait for the movie, unless the book is a comic book!

Appendix

Abby: That's funny. Do you know the *Diary of a Wimpy Kid* series? Guess how many copies of those books have been sold?

Ralph: I don't know… one hundred thousand?

Abby: No higher!

Ralph: Five hundred thousand!

Abby: Higher!

Ralph: [impressed] One million.

Abby: Two HUNDRED million!! Guess how many copies of *Narnia* have been sold?

Ralph: I don't know…

Abby: 100 million! *Lord of the Rings* – 150 million! *The Harry Potter series* – 500 million. And guess what else! Over five BILLION copies of the

Bible have been sold! Every year 100 million copies of the Bible are sold or given away. In fact, it's been translated into more languages than any other book in history! Did you know the *YouVersion Bible App* has been downloaded more than 250 million times, in 1,000 languages?! The Bible is the best-selling book of the year every year!!!

Ralph: Wow!! I bet no one knows that! I'm going to have to make a new post… [He types while talking out loud]. Hey everyone, I bet you didn't know that the Bible is the best-selling book? More than five BILLION copies… [His voice fades.]

END

Appendix

Skit-Lesson 5

Two characters: **Joseph and Juan**

Joseph: Juan, my dad is so annoying!

Juan: Why? What did he do?

Joseph: He expects me to be perfect all the time. When I mess up, he gets upset. I'm not Superman!

Juan: You mean Super Kid!

Joseph: Come on Juan, I'm being serious.

Juan: Okay, sorry. My dad is like that too. He says he pushes me to do well because he loves me. It's a parent thing.

Joseph: I guess (sigh). My dad always complains that I watch TV too much or play video games. He says [say in a mockingly stern way], "Learn something, Joseph. You were born for a reason, you know! You were not born to sit around all day doing nothing." I was born for a reason?! Nobody told me about the reason.

Juan: I guess dads can be a bit annoying, or downright scary at times, but sometimes dads can be cool.

Joseph: Ugh!

Juan: But still, I know my dad loves me because he is the first person to run to my rescue if I am hurt. If I have a problem, I can talk to him about it. Sometimes he tells me that I need to make better choices. I swear he has eyes in the back of his head. He seems to know every time I mess up!

Joseph: But why do dads have to care about everything we do? Why can't they just leave us alone sometimes?

Juan: I know, right? It's annoying, but at least your dad cares. Angela's dad took off months ago and she hasn't heard from him since. He doesn't have any idea what she is doing. She wishes he cared enough to at least check in once in a while.

Joseph: Yeah (sigh), I guess you're right. [Joseph gets up to leave.] Later, Juan. I am off to have a man-to-man talk with my dad.

Juan: You mean man to boy!

Joseph: Ugh! [waves goodbye]

END

Made in the USA
Columbia, SC
24 July 2021